Anonymus

A manual for the members of the Sodality of the Blessed Virgin Mary

Anonymus

A manual for the members of the Sodality of the Blessed Virgin Mary

ISBN/EAN: 9783742840714

Manufactured in Europe, USA, Canada, Australia, Japa

Cover: Foto ©Lupo / pixelio.de

Manufactured and distributed by brebook publishing software
(www.brebook.com)

Anonymus

A manual for the members of the Sodality of the Blessed Virgin Mary

A MANUAL

—FOR THE MEMBERS OF THE—

SODALITY

—OF THE—

BLESSED VIRGIN MARY.

———

Affiliated to the Mother Sodality
in Rome.

———

BALTIMORE :
ST. MARY'S INDUSTRIAL SCHOOL STEAM PRESS.

——

1892.

RULES OF THE SODALITY OF THE BLESSED VIRGIN MARY.

I.

Since it is from the Most Blessed Virgin, Mother of God, principal patroness of this Sodality, we are to expect patronage and protection—as she is Mother of Mercy, loving those that love her, guardian and protectress of those who piously and religiously seek her aid—it is of the highest importance that the members of the same Sodality should not only greatly venerate and in a very special manner honor her, but also seek by the blameless conduct of their lives, to imitate the example of her wonderful virtues, and to excite each other to love her.

The accomplishment of all this will be greatly facilitated by the observance of the rules of the Sodality.

II.

The end of the Sodality is to increase in virtue and Christian piety; therefore to attain this end the frequentation of the Sacraments is of the greatest necessity. Those who belong to the Sodality should receive the sacraments of Penance and of Holy Eucharist at least once a month.

III.

The members of the Sodality should attend regularly each and every meeting of the Sodality and should never absent themselves without a good and sufficient reason.

IV.

GOOD WORKS RECOMMENDED.

1. *Every day :* To begin the day by some special prayer to their heavenly Patroness as the Memorare. In the Prima Primaria three Hail Marys are prescribed, morning and night.

To be present, if possible, at the Holy Sacrifice of the Mass.

To give some time to meditation on heavenly things or spiritual reading.

To recite, at least in part, the rosary or the office of the Blessed Virgin.

To examine one's conscience before retiring to rest

2. *Once a month*, at the very least, to approach the sacraments of Penance and the Eucharist.

8. At the death of a Sodalist to accompany the body to the grave, and fervently command the soul to God.

4. At all times to be energetic in furthering whatever tends to the increase and well-being of the Church and of religion, to strive earnestly by example, as well as by words, to lead back to the way of salvation wanderers from the faith or from the path of Christian virtue, to practice diligently the works of mercy, especially towards Sodalists in time of sickness: finally to strive to acquire not only those virtues which no Christian can be without, but to vie with each other in piety, purity, humility, modesty, diligence and industry in the discharge of the duties of one's state of life.

V.

FRATERNAL UNION AND CHARITY.

Let them all love one another with true and sincere charity, and be careful to preserve peace and fraternal concord, and, day after day, to advance in the practice of true and Christian virtue. They will be greatly assisted to the attainment of this end by frequenting the meetings of the Sodality, by not neglecting its pious exercises, by often seeking the society of those whose conversation may be useful, by avoiding bad company, and all occasions that might in any way be injurious, as, for example, plays, quarrels, strifes, complaints, and other things of the kind that would injure the good name and reputation of the Sodality. Let them, on the contrary, try so to bear themselves on all occasions as to be thought worthy of being under the special protection of the Most Blessed Virgin.

PUBLIC READING OF THE RULES OF THE SODALITY.

That these laws and constitutions may the more easily be kept, let them be publicly read at the meeting of the Sodality once a month instead of the usual instruction.

ORDER OF CEREMONIES

—FOR—

SOLEMN RECEPTION.

I.

HYMN.

VENI CREATOR

1. Come, O Creator Spirit blest,
   And in our souls take up Thy rest :
   Come, with thy grace and heavenly aid,
   And fill the hearts which Thou hast made.

   *   *   *   *   *   *   *

7. All glory while the ages run
   Be to the Father, and the Son :
   Who rose from death ; like praise to thee,
   O Holy Ghost, eternally.   Amen.

II.

The Celebrant says in a loud voice.—For the greater praise and glory of the Most Holy Trinity, for the honor of the most Blessed Virgin Mary, conceived without sin, our Mother and our Patroness, for the increase of our Sodality, let those who wish to be admitted come forward.

Then the Candidates come foward to the altar rail as their names are called out.

When at the rail the Celebrant says.—Do you desire to be received into the Sodality of the Blessed Virgin and devote yourselves wholly herein to our Saviour Jesus under the protection of the most glorious Virgin Mary your Mother?

Candidates.—We desire it with all our hearts.

Celebrant.—Do you sincerely purpose to endeavor, by your devotion in this Sodality, to promote love for piety, to increase fraternal charity, and by your good example to give edification to your neighbor?

Candidates.—We desire it.

Celebrant.—Do you promise to observe the rules of the Sodality, to pay filial respect to the Directors, and to be promptly obedient to them in all that regards the Sodality?

Candidates.—We promise.

Celebrant.—And for how long a period will you observe your present promises?

Candidates.—We will observe them forever.

Celebrant.—Dearly beloved, this your desire is most acceptable to the Blessed Virgin, most beneficial to yourselves, and most important. By being devout servants and clients of the most holy Mother of God, you may expect through her intercession to receive many heavenly favors. For this most holy Mother assists those who invoke her, shelters them by her protection in the dangers, anxieties and miseries of this life, and in the hour of death never abandons those who are truly devout to her. That you also may experience this her protection, endeavor that your conduct and your whole life may prove that you have been numbered amongst her children. And that you may more faithfully fulfill what you promise, make solemnly at the feet of your most holy Mother, in presence of the whole Sodality, your Act of Consecration.

III.

Each Candidate, holding a lighted candle in his(her)hand, here recites the Act of Consecration in a clear audible voice, repeating after the Celebrant.

ACT OF CONSECRATION.

Holy Mary, Immaculate Virgin. Mother of God, I, ———,choose thee this day for my Mother, Queen, Patroness, and advocate, and I firmly reslove never to depart, either is word or action, from the duty which I owe to thee, nor to suffer those who are committed to my charge to say or do anything against thy honor, and the respect which thou deservest. Receive me, therefore, as thy devoted servant for ever, assist me in all the actions of my life, and forsake me not at the hour of my death. Amen.

IV.

BLESSING OF MEDALS.

V. Adjutorium nostrum in nomine Domini.
R. Qui fecit ocelum et terrem.
V. Domine exaudi orationem meam.
R. Et clamor meus ad te veniat.
V. Dominus vobiscum.
R. Et cum spiritu tuo.

OREMUS.

OMNIPOTENS sempiterne Deus, qui sanctorum tuorum imagines (sive effigies) sculpi aut pingi non reprobas, ut quoties illas oculis corporis intuemur, toties eorum actus et sanctitatem ad imitandem memoriæ oculis meditemur ; has quæsumus, imagines in honorem et memoriam beatissimæ Virginis Mariæ, Matris Domini nostri Jesu Christi, adaptatas bene✠dicere et sancti✠ficare digneris, et præsta, ut quicumque coram illis.

Then the Celebrant invests with the medal, and hands the Sodality manual to each candidate saying:

Receive this medal and manual of the Blessed Virgin Mary as a safeguard and defence for your body and soul, that by the grace of God and the assistance of Mary your Mother you may desire to obtain eternal happiness in the name of the Father and of the Son and of the Holy Ghost. Amen.

Then the Celebrant ascending to the platform of the Altar reads aloud :

To the greater glory of God, and to the honor of the Blessed Virgin Mary, and for the spiritual good of this Sodality, and by the power granted me by our most Holy Father the Pope [*N. N.*] I, [*N. N.*] Director for the time being of this Sodality, receive you [*N. N.*], into the number of the members of our Sodality, erected under the title of the (* * * *), and render you sharers and declare you partakers of all the graces and fruits, privileges, and indulgences which the Holy Roman Church has granted to the Primary Sodality at Rome to which ours has been canonically affiliated : In the name of the Father ✠ and of the Son ✠ and of the Holy ✠ Ghost. Amen.

May Christ receive you into the number of our brethren and His servants. May He give you grace to lead a holy life, opportunity to do good, and constancy to persevere therein, that you may arrive happily at the inheritance of life eternal. And as fraternal charity unites us this day spiritually on earth, may the Divine Goodness, who is the author and lover of charity, vouchsafe to admit us among the saints in heaven. Through the same Christ our Lord. Amen.

Then kneeling at the foot of the Altar, the Celebrant continues, being answered by all the members of the Sodality.

V.   Confirm O Lord what Thou hast wrought in us.

R.   From Thy holy temple which is in Jerusalem.

V. Save thy servants.

R. Who hope in Thee, O my God.

V. Send them help from Thy holy place.

R. And from Sin protect them.

V. Lord hear my prayer.

R. And let my cry come unto Thee.

V. Lord be with you.

R. And with thy spirit.

LET US PRAY.

Hear O Lord, our supplication and deign to bless these Thy servants whom we have received into the Sodality of the Most Blessed Virgin Mary : and grant that by the aid of Thy grace they may share the rules, live holy and piously and may by keeping them merit eternal life. *Amen.*

After the ceremony the new members return to their alloted places.

PRAYER BEFORE RECITATION OF THE OFFICE.

Open, O Lord, our mouths to bless Thy holy Name, cleanse our hearts from all vain and distracting thoughts, enlighten our understandings, inflame our wills that we may worthily perform this holy Office with attention and devotion, and may deserve to be heard in the presence of Thy Divine Majesty, Who with the Father and Holy Ghost, livest and reignest, one God, world without end. Amen.

We offer up this holy Office and unite our intentions with those of Jesus Christ, Thy Son, Who, whilst on earth, rendered Thee a most acceptable homage of divine praise.

PRAYER AFTER THE RECITATION OF THE OFFICE.

To the most holy and undivided Trinity, to the humanity of our Lord Jesus Christ crucified, to the fruitful purity of the most blessed and glorious ever Virgin Mary, and to all the Saints, be everlasting praise, honor, virtue and glory from every creature; and to us the remission of all our sins, for ever and ever.

R. Amen.

V. Blessed is the womb of the Virgin Mary that bore the Son of the eternal Father.

R. And blessed are the breasts that gave suck to Christ the Lord.

Our Father. Hail Mary.

VESPERS.

Hail Mary, &c.

V. O GOD, come to my assistance.

R. O Lord, make haste to help me.

V. Glory be to the Father, and to the Son, and to the Holy Ghost.

R. As it was in the beginning is now, and ever shall be, world without end. *Amen.*

Ant. While the king.

PSALM CIX.

The Lord said to my Lord : Sit Thou at my right hand :

Until I make Thy enemies Thy foot-stool.

The Lord will send forth the sceptre of Thy power out of Sion : rule Thou in the midst of Thy enemies.

With Thee is the principality in the day of Thy strength ; in the brightness of the Saints : from the womb before the day star I begot Thee.

The Lord hath sworn, and He will not repent : thou art a priest forever according to the order of Melchisedech.

The Lord at Thy right hand hath broken kings in the day of His wrath.

He shall judge among nations, He shall fill ruins : He shall crush the heads in the land of many.

He shall drink of the torrent in the. way, therefore shall He lift up His head.

Glory be to the Father, &c.

Ant. While the king was at his repose, my spikenard sent forth its odor.

Ant. His left hand.

PSALM CXII.

Praise the Lord, ye children : praise ye the name of the Lord.

Blessed be the name of the Lord from hence forth now and forever.

From the rising of the sun unto the going down of the same, the name of the Lord is worthy of praise.

The Lord is high above all nations : and His glory above the heavens.

Who is as the Lord our God, Who dwelleth on high : and looketh down on the low things in heaven and on earth.

Raising up the needy from the earth, and lifting up the poor from the dunghill.

That he may place him with princes, with the princes of his people.

Who maketh the barren woman to dwell in a house, the joyful mother of children.

Glory be to the Father, &c.

Ant. His left hand is under my head and His right hand shall embrace me.

Ant. I am black but beautiful.

PSALM CXXI.

I rejoiced at the things that were said to me : we shall go into the house of the Lord.

Our feet were standing in thy courts, O Jerusalem.

Jerusalem, which is built as a city, which is compact together.

For thither did the tribes go up, the tribes of the Lord ; the testimony of Israel, to praise the name of the Lord.

Because there seats have sat in Judgment, seats upon the house of David.

Pray ye for the things that are for the peace of Jerusalem : and abundance for them that love thee.

Let peace be in thy strength : and abundance in thy towers.

For the sake of my brethren and of my neighbors, I spoke peace of thee.

Because of the house of the Lord our God, I have sought good things for thee.

Glory be to the Father, &c.

Ant. I am black but beautiful, O ye daughters of Jerusalem ! therefore the king hath loved me, and brought me into his house.

Ant. Winter is now past.

Psalm cxxvi.

Unless the Lord build the house, they labor in vain that build it.

Unless the Lord keep the city, he watcheth in vain that keepeth it.

It is in vain for you to rise before light: rise ye after you have sitten, you that eat the bread of sorrow.

When He shall give sleep to His beloved : behold, the inheritance of the Lord are children : the reward, the fruit of the womb.

As arrows in the hand of the mighty, so the children of them that have been shaken.

Blessed is the man that has filled his desire with them ; he shall not be confounded when he shall speak to his enemies in the gate.

Glory be to the Father, &c.

Ant. Winter is now past, the rain is over and gone ; arise, my love, and come.

Ant. Thou art beautiful.

Psalm cxlvii.

Praise the Lord O Jerusalam : praise thy God, O Sion.

Because He hath strengthened the bolts of thy gates, He hath blessed thy children within thee.

Who hath placed peace in thy borders : and fillith thee with the fat of corn.

Who sendeth forth His speech to the earth
His word runneth swiftly.

Who giveth snow like wool : scattereth mists
like ashes.

He sendeth His crystal like morsels : who
shall stand before the face of His cold ?

He shall send out His word, and shall melt
them : His winds shall blow, and the waters
shall run.

Who declareth His word to Jacob : His jus-.
tices and His judgements to Israel.

He hath not done in like manner to every
nation : and His judgments He hath not made
manifest to them.   Alleluia.

Glory be to the Father, &c.

Ant. Thou art beautiful and sweet in thy
delights, O holy Mother of God !

CHAPTER.   ECCL. XXIV.

From the beginning, and before the world
was I created, and unto the world to come I
shall not cease to be, and in the holy dwelling
place I have ministered before Him.

R. Thanks be to God.

AVE MARIS STELLA.

Gentle star of ocean!
  Portal of the sky!
Ever Virgin Mother
  Of the Lord most high!

Oh, by Gabriel's Ave,
  Utter'd long ago,
Eva's name reversing,
  'Stablish peace below;

Break the captive's fetters!
  Light on blindness pour
All our ills expelling,
  Every bliss implore. .

Show thyself a Mother;
  Offer Him our sighs,
Who for us incarnate,
  Did not thee despise.

Virgin of all virgins!
  To thy shelter take us,
Gentlest of the gentle!
  Chaste and gentle make us.

Still as on our journey,
  Help our weak endeavor,
Till with Thee and Jesus
  We rejoice forever.

Through the highest heaven,
  To the Almighty Three,
Father, Son, and Spirit,
  One same glory be.

V. Grace is poured abroad in thy lips.

R. Therefore hath God blessed thee forever.

Ant. O blessed Mother.

CANTICLE OF THE BLESSED VIRGIN.
Luke 1.

My soul doth magnify the Lord :

And my spirit hath rejoiced in God my Saviour.

Because He hath regarded the humility of His handmaid : for behold from henceforth all generations shall call me blessed.

Because He that is mighty hath done great things to me : and holy is His name.

And His mercy is from generation unto generations, to them that fear Him.

He hath showed might in His arm ; He hath scattered the proud in the conceit of their heart.

He hath put down the mighty from their seat and hath exalted the humble.

He hath filled the hungry with good things : and the rich He hath sent away empty.

He hath received His servant Israel : being mindful of His mercy.

As He spoke to our fathers : to Abraham and to his seed forever.

Glory be to the Father, &c.

Ant. O blessed mother, and ever virgin, glorious queen of the world, make intercession for us to our Lord.

V. Lord hear my prayer.

R. And let my cry come to Thee.

LET US PRAY.

Lord God ! we beseech Thee, grant that we Thy servants may enjoy perpetual health for mind and body ; and that, by the glorious intercession of the ever blessed Virgin Mary, we may pass from this present sorrow to the enjoyment of everlasting gladness : through our Lord, &c. Amen.

COMMEMORATION OF THE SAINTS.

Ant. All ye Saints of God, vouchsafe to make intercession for our salvation and that of all.

V. Be glad in the Lord and rejoice ye just.

R. And glory all ye right of heart.

LET US PRAY.

Protect, O Lord, Thy people, and let the confidence we have in the intercession of the blessed Apostles Peter and Paul and of Thy other apostles, pervail with Thee to perserve and defend us forever. May all Thy Saints, O Lord, we beseech Thee, everywhere assist us, that whilst we ce'ebrate their merits, we may be sensible of their protection. Grant us Thy peace in our times, and repel all wickedness from Thy Church; prosperously guide the steps, actions and desires of us and all Thy servants in the way of salvation; give eternal blessings to those who have done good to us, and everlasting rest to the faithful departed; through the Lord Jesus Christ, thy Son. Amen.

V. Lord. hear my prayer.

R. And let my cry come to Thee.

V. Let us bless the Lord.

R. Thanks be to God.

V. May the souls of the faithful departed through the mercy of God rest in peace.

R. Amen.

COMPLINE.

Hail Mary.

Convert us, O God, our Saviour.

R. And turn off Thy anger from us.

V. O God, come to my assistance.

R. O Lord, make haste to help me.

Glory be to the Father, &c.

PSALM CXXVIII.

Often have they fought against me from my youth : let Israel now say.

Often have they fought against me from my youth : but they could not pervail over me.

The wicked have wrought upon my back, they have lengthened their iniquity.

The Lord who is just will cut the necks of sinners : let them all be confounded and turned back, that hate Sion.

Let them be as grass upon the tops of houses, which withereth before it be plucked up.

Wherewith the mower filleth not his hand, nor he that gathereth sheaves, his bosom.

And they that passed by have not said : The blessing of the Lord be upon you : we have blessed you in the name of the Lord.

Glory be to the Father, &c.

PSALM CXXIX.

Out of the depths I have cried to thee, O Lord : Lord hear my voice.

Let Thy ears be attentive to the voice of my supplication.

If Thou, O Lord, wilt mark iniquities ; Lord, who shall stand it ?

For with Thee there is merciful forgiveness : and by reason of Thy law, I have waited for Thee, O Lord.

My soul hath relied on His word ; my soul hath hoped in the Lord.

From the morning watch even until night, let Israel hope in the Lord.

Because with the Lord there is mercy ; and with him plentiful redemption.

And he shall redeem Israel from all his iniquities.

Glory be to the Father, &c.

PSALM CXXX.

Lord, my heart is not exalted : nor are my eyes lofty.

Neither have I walked in great matters, nor in wonderful things above me.

If I was not humble minded, but exalted my soul :

As a child that is weaned is toward his mother, so reward in my soul.

Let Israel hope in the Lord, from henceforth now and forever.

Glory be to the Father, &c.

HYMN.

Remember, O Creator Lord !
　That in the Virgin's sacred womb,
Thou wast conceived, and of her flesh,
　Didst our mortality assume.

Mother of Grace, O Mary blest !
　To thee, sweet fount of love we fly ;
Shield us through life, and take us hence,
　To thy dear bosom when we die.

O Jesus ! born of Virgin bright,
　Immortal giory be to Thee ;
Praise to the Father infinite,
　And Holy Ghost eternally.

Chapter. ECCLES. XXIV.

I am the Mother of fair love, and of fear, and of knowledge, and of holy hope.

R. Thanks be to God.

V. Pray for us, Mother of God.

R. That we may be made worthy of the promises of Christ.

Ant. Under Thy protection.

CANTICLE OF SIMEON. *Luke* II.

Now Thou dost dismiss Thy servant, O Lord, according to Thy word, in peace ; because my eyes have seen Thy salvation, which Thou hast prepared before the face of all people, a light to the revelation of the Gentiles, and the glory of Thy people Israel.

Glory be to the Father, &c.

Ant. Under Thy protection we take our refuge, O holy Mother of God ! despise not our petitions in our necessities but ever deliver us from all dangers, O glorious and blessed Virgin !

Lord have mercy on us. Christ have mercy on us. Lord have mercy on us.

V. Lòrd, hear my prayer.

R. And let my cry come to Thee.

LET US PRAY.

We beseech Thee, O Lord, that the glorious intercession of the ever blessed and glorious Virgin Mary may protect us, and bring us to life everlasting, through our Lord Jesus Christ, Thy Son, Who, &c.

R. Amen.

V. Lord, hear my prayer.

R. And let my cry come to Thee.

V. Let us bless the Lord.

R. Thanks be to God.

BLESSING.

May the almighty and merciful Lord, Father, and Son, and Holy Ghost, bless and keep us.

R. Amen.

ANTHEM.

Hail ! Holy Queen, Mother of mercy, our life our sweetness, and our hope ! To thee do we cry, poor banished children of Eve ; to thee do we send up our sighs, mourning and weeping in this valley of tears ! Turn, then, most gracious Advocate, thine eyes of mercy toward us and after this our exile, show unto us, the blessed fruit of thy womb, Jesus. O clement, O loving, O sweet Virgin Mary :

V. Pray for us, O holy Mother of God !

R. That we may be made worthy of the promises of Christ.

LET US PRAY.

Almighty and eternal God, who by the co-operation of the Holy Ghost, didst prepare the body and soul of the glorious Virgin Mother, Mary, that she might become a worthy habitation for Thy Son, grant, that as with joy we celebrate her memory, so by her pious intercession we may be delivered from present evils and eternal death : through the same Christ, our Lord.

R. Amen.

V. May the Divine assistance always remain with us.

R. Amen.

PRIME.

Ave Maria, &c.

V. O God, come to my assistance.

R. O Lord, make haste to help me.

V. Glory be to the Father, &c.

R. As it was in the beginning, &c.

HYMN.

REMEMBER, O Creator, Lord !
That in the Virgin's sacred womb
Thou wast conceived, and of her flesh
Didst our mortality assume.

Mother of grace, O Mary blest !
To thee, sweet fount of love, we fly ;
Shield us through life, and take us hence
To thy dear bosom when we die.

O Jesus ! born of Virgin bright,
Immortal glory be to Thee,
Praise to the Father infinite,
And Holy Ghost eternally.

Ant. Mary is taken up:

PSALM LIII.

SAVE me, O God, by Thy name, and judge me in Thy strength.

O God, hear my prayer ; give ear to the words of my mouth.

For strangers have risen up against me; and the mighty have sought after my soul; and they have not set God before their eyes.

For behold, God is my helper : and the Lord is the protector of my soul.

Turn back the evils upon my enemies : and cut them off in Thy truth.

I will freely sacrifice to Thee, and will give praise, O God, to Thy name : because it is good.

For Thou hast delivered me out of all trouble ; and my eye hath looked down upon my enemies.

Glory be to the Father, &c.

PSALM LXXXIV.

LORD, Thou hast blessed Thy land ; Thou hast turned away the captivity of Jacob.

Thou hast forgiven the iniquity of Thy people ; Thou hast covered all their sins.

Thou hast mitigated all Thy anger ; Thou hast turned away from the wrath of Thy indignation.

Convert us, O God our Saviour : and turn off Thy anger from us.

Wilt Thou be angry with us forever : or wilt Thou extend Thy wrath from generation to generation ?

Thou wilt turn, O God, and bring us to life : and Thy people shall rejoice in Thee.

Show us, O Lord, Thy mercy ; and grant us Thy salvation.

I will hear what the Lord God will speak in me; for he will speak peace unto His people and unto His saints: and unto them that are converted to the heart.

Surely His salvation is near to them that fear Him: that glory may dwell in our land.

Mercy and truth have meet each other: justice and peace have kissed.

Truth is sprung out of the earth: and justice hath looked down from heaven.

For the Lord will give goodness: and our earth shall yield her fruit.

Justice shall walk before Him, and shall set His steps in the way.

Glory be to the Father, &c.

PSALM CXVI.

O praise the Lord all ye nations: praise Him all ye people.

For His mercy is confirmed upon us: and the truth of the Lord remaineth forever.

Glory be to the Father, &c.

Ant. Mary is taken up into heaven; the angels rejoice, and with praises bless our Lord.

Chapter. CANT. VI.

WHO is she that cometh forth as the morning rising, fair as the moon, bright as the sun, terrible as an army set in array.

R. Thanks be to God.

V. Vouchsafe O sacred Virgin, to accept my praises.

R. Give me power against thy enemies.

Lord, have mercy on us. Christ, have mercy on us. Lord, have mercy on us.

V. Lord, hear my prayer.

R. And let my cry come to Thee.

LET US PRAY.

O GOD, who wast pleased to make choice of the chaste womb of the Blessed Virgin Mary for Thy abode, grant, we beseech thee, that being protected by the assistance of her intercession, we may celebrate her memory with spiritual joy : who livest and reignest with God the Father.

V. Lord, hear my prayer.

R. And let my cry come to Thee.

V. Let us bless the Lord.

R. Thanks be to God.

V. May the souls of the faithful departed, through the mercy of God, rest in peace.

R. Amen.

TIERCE.

Hail Mary, &c.

V. O God come to my assistance.

R. O Lord make haste to help me.

Glory be to the Father, &c.

HYMN.

REMEMBER. O Creator Lord !
   That in the Virgin's sacred womb
Thou was conceived, and of her flesh
   Didst our mortality assume.

Mother of grace. O Mary blest !
   To thee sweet fount of love we fly,
Shield us through life, and take us hence
   To thy dear bosom when we die.

O Jesus ! born of Virgin bright,
   Immortal glory be to Thee,
Praise to the Father infinite,
   And holy Ghost eternally.

Ant. The Virgin Mary.

PSALM CXIX.

In my trouble, I cried to the Lord ; and He heard me.

O Lord, deliver my soul from wicked lips, and a deceitful tongue.

What shall be given to thee, or what shall be added to thee, to a deceitful tongue?

The sharp arrows of the mighty, with coals that lay waste.

Wo is me, that my sojourning is prolonged I have dwelt with the inhabitants of Cedar : my soul hath been long a sojourner.

With them that hated peace I was peaceable: when I spoke to them they fought against Me without cause.

Glory be to the Father, &c.

PSALM CXX.

I HAVE lifted up my eyes to the mountains, from whence help shall come to me.

My help is from the Lord, Who made heaven and earth.

May he not suffer thy foot to be moved neither let him slumber that keepeth thee.

Behold, He shall neither slumber nor sleep that keepeth Israel.

The Lord is thy keeper : the Lord is thy protection upon thy right hand.

The sun shall not burn thee by day ; nor the moon by night.

The Lord keepeth thee from all evil : may the Lord keep thy soul.

May the Lord keep thy coming in and thy going out : from henceforth now and forever.

Glory be to the Father, &c.

PSALM CXXI.

I REJOICED at the things that were said to me :
We shall go into the house of the Lord.

Our feet were standing in thy courts, O
Jerusalem.

Jerusalem, which is built as a city, which is
compact together.

For thither did the tribes go up, the tribes
of the Lord ; the testimony of Israel, to praise
the name of the Lord.

Because there seats have sat in judgment,
seats upon the house of David.

Pray ye for the things that are for the peace
of Jerusalem ; and abundance for them that
love thee.

Let peace be in thy strength : and abundance
in thy towers.

For the sake of my brethren and of my
neighbors, I spoke peace of thee.

Because of the house of the Lord our God,
I have sought good things for thee.

Glory be to the Father, &c.

Ant. The Virgin Mary is taken up to the
heavenly chamber, in which the King of kings
sits on His starry throne.

Chapter. ECCLES. XXIV.

And so was I established in Sion, and in the
holy city likewise I rested : and my power was
in Jerusalem.

R. Thanks be to God.

V. Grace is poured abroad in thy lips.

R. Therefore hath God blessed thee forever.

Lord have mercy on us. Chirst have mercy on us. Lord have mercy on us.

V. Lord, hear my prayer.

R. And let my cry come to Thee.

LET US PRAY.

O God, Who by the fruitful virginity of the blessed Virgin Mary, hast given to mankind the rewards of eternal salvation, grant, we beseech Thee, that we may be sensible of the benefit of her intercession, by whom we have received the author of life, our Lord Jesus Chirst, Thy Son ; who liveth and reigneth in one, &c.

R. Amen.

V. Lord, hear my prayer.

R. And let my cry come to Thee.

V. Let us bless God.

R. Thanks be to God.

V. May the souls of the faithful departed through the mercy of God, rest in peace.

R. Amen.

OFFICE FOR THE DEAD.

VESPERS.

Ant. I will please.

PSALM CXIV.

I have loved, because the Lord will hear the voice of my prayer.

Because He hath inclined His ear unto me : and in my days I will call upon Him.

The sorrows of death have compassed me, and the perils of hell have found me.

I met with trouble and sorrow ; and I called upon the name of the Lord.

O Lord deliver my soul : the Lord is merciful and just, and our God showeth mercy.

The Lord is the keeper of little ones : I was humbled and He delivered me.

Turn, O my soul, into thy rest : for the Lord hath been bountiful to thee.

For He hath delivered my soul from death : my eyes from tears, my feet from falling.

I will please the Lord in the land of the living.

Eternal rest grant to them, O Lord.

And let perpetual light shine upon them.

Ant. I will please the Lord in the land of the living.

Ant. Wo is me, O Lord.

PSALM CXIX.

In my trouble, I cried to the Lord; and **He** heard me.

O Lord, deliver my soul from wicked lips, and a deceitful tongue.

What shall be given to thee, or what shall be added to thee, to a deceitful tongue?

The sharp arrows of the mighty, with coals that lay waste.

Wo is me, that my sojourning is prolonged: I have dwelt with the inhabitants of Cedar my soul hath been long a sojourner.

With them that hated peace I was peaceable: when I spoke to them they fought against **Me** without cause.

Eternal rest, &c.

Ant. Wo is me, O Lord, that my sojourning is prolonged.

Ant. The Lord keepeth thee.

PSALM CXX.

I have lifted up my eyes to the mountains, whence help shall come to me.

My help is from the Lord, who made heaven and earth.

May he not suffer thy foot to be moved neither let him slumber that keepeth thee.

Behold, He shall neither slumber nor sleep, that keepeth Israel.

The Lord is thy keeper : the Lord is thy protection upon the right hand.

The sun shall not burn thee by day ; nor the moon by night.

The Lord keepeth thee from all evil, may the Lord keep thy soul.

May the Lord keep thy coming in and thy going out : from henceforth now and forever.

Eternal rest, &c.

Ant. The Lord keepeth thee from all evil : may the Lord keep thy soul.

Ant. If thou, O Lord.

PSALM CXXIX.

Out of the depths I have cried to Thee, O Lord : Lord, hear my voice.

Let Thy ears be attentive to the voice of my supplication.

If Thou O Lord, wilt mark iniquities: Lord, who shall stand it.

For with Thee there is merciful forgiveness; and by reason of Thy law, I have waited for Thee, O Lord.

My soul hath relied on His word: my soul hath hoped in the Lord.

From the morning watch even until night let Israel hope in the Lord.

Because with the Lord there is mercy: and with Him plentiful redemption.

And He shall redeem Israel from all his iniquities.

Eternal rest, &c.

Ant. If Thou, O Lord, wilt mark iniquites, Lord, who shall stand it?

Ant. Despise not, O Lord.

PSALM CXXXVII.

I will praise Thee, O Lord, with my whole heart: for Thou hast heard the words of my mouth.

I will sing praise to Thee in the sight of the angels: I will worship towards Thy holy temple, and I will give glory to Thy name:

For Thy mercy and for Thy truth: for Thou hast magnified Thy holy name above all.

In what day soever I shall call upon Thee, hear me; Thou shalt multiply strength in my soul.

May all the kings of the earth give glory to Thee ; for they have heard all the words of Thy mouth.

And let them sing in the ways of the Lord ; for great is the glory of the Lord.

For the Lord is high, and looketh on the low ; and the high He knoweth afar off.

If I shall walk in the midst of tribulation, Thou will quicken me: and Thou hast stretched forth Thy hand against the wrath of my enemies ; and Thy right hand hath saved me.

The Lord will repay for me ; Thy mercy O Lord, endureth forever ; O despise not the works of Thy hands.

Eternal rest, &c.

Ant. Despise not, O Lord, the works of Thy hands.

V. I heard a voice from heaven saying to me.

R. Blessed are the dead who die in the Lord.

Ant. All that the Father giveth me.

The Canticle of the BLESSED VIRGIN.

My soul doth magnify: the Lord.

And my spirit hath rejoiced; in God my Saviour.

For He hath regarded the humility of His handmaid; for behold from henceforth all generations shall call me blessed.

For He that is mighty hath done great things unto me; and holy is His name.

And His mercy is from generation to generation; unto them that fear Him.

He hath showed strength with His arm; He hath scattered the proud in the imagination of their heart.

He hath put down the mighty from their seat; and hath exalted the humble.

He hath filled the hungry with good things; and the rich he hath sent empty away.

He hath upholden His servant Israel; being mindful of His mercy.

As He spake unto our fathers; to Abraham and his seed forever.

Eternal rest, &c.

Ant. All that the Father giveth me shall come to me; and him that cometh to me I will not cast him out.

The following prayers are said kneeling.

Our Father, &c., *in silence.*

V. And lead us not into temptation

R. But deliver us from evil.

PSALM CXLV.

Praise the Lord, O my soul; in my life I will praise the Lord : I will sing to my God as long as I shall be.

Put not your trust in princes, in the children of men, in whom there is no salvation.

His spirit shall go forth; and he shall return into his earth : in that day all their thoughts shall perish.

Blessed is he who hath the God of Jacob for his helper, whose hope is in the Lord his God: who made heaven and earth, the sea, and all things that are in them.

Who keepeth truth forever ; Who executeth judgment for them that suffer wrong; Who giveth food to the hungry.

The Lord looseth them that are fettered ; the Lord enlighteneth the blind.

The Lord lifteth up them that are cast down: the Lord loveth the just.

The Lord keepeth the strangers: He will support the fatherless and the widow: and the ways of sinners He will destroy.

The Lord shall reign forever : thy God, O Sion, unto generation and generation.

Eternal rest, &c.

V. From the gate of hell.

R. Deliver their souls, O Lord.

V. May they rest in peace.

R. Amen.

V. Lord, hear my prayer.

R. And let my cry come to Thee !

V. The Lord be with you.

R. And with thy spirit.

PRAYER SAID AFTER THE DECEASE OF A SODALIST.

Absolve, we beseech Thee, O Lord, the soul of Thy servant N. that being dead to the world, he(*or* she)may live to Thee ; and whatever he (*or* she)has committed through human frailty, do Thou wipe away by the pardon of Thy most merciful goodness ; through our Lord Jesus Christ Thy Son, who livest and reignest with Thee in the unity of the Holy Ghost, God, world without end.

R. Amen.

FOR SODALISTS DECEASED.

Incline, O Lord, Thy ear to our prayers, in which we humbly beseech Thy mercy, that Thou wouldst place the souls of Thy servants, which Thou hast caused to depart from this world, in the region of peace and light, and unite them in the fellowship of Thy saints : through, &c.

R. Amen.

V. Eternal rest grant to them, O Lord.

R. And let perpetual light shine upon them.

V. May they rest in peace.

R. Amen.

BENEDICTION.

HYMN.

1. O Saving Victim, opening wide
    The gate of Heaven to man below!
  Our foes press on from every side;
    Thine aid supply, Thy strength bestow.

2. To Thy great name be endless praise,
    Immortal Godhead: One in Three!
  O grant us endless length of days
    In our true native land with Thee!

Tantum ergo Sacramentum
  Veneremur cernui :
Et antiquum documentum
  Novo cedat ritui,
Præstet fides supplementum
  Sensuum defectui,

Genitori, Genitoque
  Laus et jubilatio,
Salus, honor virtus quoque
  Sit et benedictio :
Procedenti ab utroque
  Compar sit laudatio.   Amen.

V.   Panem de cœlo præstitisti eis.

R.   Omne delectamentum in se habentem.

(*Easter time and Corpus Christi*, Alleluia.)

AFTER BENEDICTION.

Te Deum.

1.   Holy God, we praise Thy name !
   Lord of all, we bow before Thee !
   All on earth Thy sceptre claim,
   All in Heaven above adore Thee :
   Infinite Thy vast domain,
   Everlasting is Thy reign.

2.   Holy Father, Holy Son,
   Holy Spirit, Three we name Thee,
   While in essence, only One.
   Undivided God, we claim Thee;
   And adoring bend the knee,
   While we own the mystery.

THE LITANY OF LORETTO.

Kyrie eleison.	Lord, have mercy on us.
Christe eleison.	Christ, have mercy on us.
Kyrie eleison.	Lord, have mercy on us.
Christe audi nos.	Christ hear us.
Christe exaudi nos.	Christ, graciously hear us.
Pater de cœlis Deus, miserere nobis.	God the Father of heaven, have mercy on us.
Fili Redemptor mundi Deus, miserere nobis.	God the Son, Redeemer of the world, have mercy on us.
Spiritus Sancta Deus, miserere nobis.	God the Holy Ghost, have mercy on us.
Sancta Trinitas. unus Deus miserere nobis.	Holy Trinity, one God, have mercy on us

Latin (Ora pro nobis.)	English (Pray for us.)
Sancta Maria,	Holy Mary, pray for us.
Sancta Dei genetrix,	Holy Mother of God.
Sancta Virgo virginum,	Holy Virgin of virgins,
Mater Christi,	Mother of Christ,
Mater divinæ gratiæ,	Mother of divine grace,
Mater purissima,	Mother most pure,
Mater castissima,	Mother most chaste,
Mater inviolata,	Mother inviolate,
Mater intemerata,	Mother undefiled,
Mater amabilis,	Mother most amiable,
Mater admirabilis,	Mother most admirable,
Mater Creatoris,	Mother of our Creator,
Mater Salvatoris,	Mother of our Saviour,
Virgo prudentissima,	Virgin most prudent,
Virgo veneranda,	Virgin most venerable,
Virgo prædicanda.	Virgin most renowned,
Virgo potens,	Virgin most powerful,
Virgo clemens,	Virgin most merciful,

Virgo fidelis,		Virgin most faithful,
Speculum justitiæ,		Mirror of justice,
Sedes sapientiæ,		Seat of wisdom,
Causa nostræ, lætitia,		Cause of our joy,
Vas spirituale,		Spiritual vessel,
Vas honorabile.		Vessel of honor,
Vas insigne devotionis,		Vessel of singular devotion,
Rosa mystica,		Mystical rose,
Turris Davidica,		Tower of David,
Turris eburnae,		Tower of ivory,
Domus aurea,		House of Gold,
Fœderis arca,		Ark of the covenant,
Janua cœli,		Gate of heaven,
Stella matutina,		Morning star,
Salus infirmorum,		Health of the sick,
Refugium peccatorum,	Ora pro nobis.	Refuge of sinners,
Consolatrix afflictorum.		Comfortress of the afflicted,
Auxilium Christianorum,		Help of Christians,
Regina Angelorum.		Queen of Angels,
Regina patriarcharum,		Queen of patriarchs,
Regina prophetarum,		Queen of prophets,
Regina apostolorum,		Queen of apostles,
Regina martyrum,		Queen of martyrs.
Regina confessorum,		Queen of confessors,
Regina virginum.		Queen of virgins,
Regina sanctorum omnium,		Queen of all saints,
Regina sine labe originali concepta,		Queen conceived without original sin,
Regina sanctissimi Rosarii.		Queen of the most holy Rosary,

Pray for us.

Agnus Dei, qui tollis peccata mundi, parce nobis, Domine.

Lamb of God, who takest away the sins of the world, spare us, O Lord.

Agnus Dei, qui tollis peccata mundi, exaudi nos, Domine.

Lamb of God, who takest away the sins of the world, graciouly hear us, O Lord.

Agnus Dei, qui tollis peccata mundi, miserere nobis.

Lamb of God who takest away the sins of the world, have mercy on us.

V. Ora pro nobis, sancta Dei genitrix.

V. Pray for us, O holy Mother of God.

R. Ut digni efficiamur promissionibus Christi.

R. That we may be made worthy of the promises of Christ.

LET US PRAY.

Pour forth we beseech Thee O Lord, Thy grace into our hearts, that we to whom the Incarnation of Thy Son was made known by the message of an Angel, may by His Passion and Cross be brought to the glory of His Resurrection, through the same Christ our Lord. Amen.

STABAT MATER.

1. At the Cross her station keeping,
   Stood the mournful mother weeping,
      Close to Jesus to the last.

2. Through her heart His sorrows sharing,
   All His bitter anguish bearing,
      Lo! the piercing sword had passed!

3. O, how sad, and sore distressed
   Now was she, that Mother Blessed
      Of the sole-begotten One.

4. Woe begone, with hearts prostration,
   Mother meek, the bitter Passion
      Saw she of her glorious Son.

5. Who could mark, from tears refraining,
   Christ's dear Mother uncomplaining,
      In so great a sorrow bowed?

6. Who, unmoved, behold her languish
   Underneath His Cross of anguish
      'Mid the fierce unpitying crowd?

7. For His people's sins rejected,
   She, her Jesus, unprotected,
      Saw with thorns, with scourges rent;

8. Saw her Son, from judgment taken,
   Her belov'd in death forsaken,
      Till His Spirit forth He sent.

9. Fount of love and holy sorrow,
   Mother! may my spirit borrow
      Somewhat of thy woe profound;

10. Unto Christ, with pure emotion,
      Raise my contrite heart's devotion,
        Love to read in every *wound*.

11. Those five wounds on Jesus smitten,
      Mother ! in my heart be written,
        Deep as in thine own they be :

12. Thou, my Saviour's Cross who bearest,
      Thou thy Son's rebuke who sharest,
        Let me share them both with thee

13. In the Passion of my Maker,
      Be my sinful soul partaker,
        Weep till death, and weep with thee.

     *   *   *   *   *   *   *   *

19. When in death my limbs are failing,
      Let Thy Mother's prayer prevailing
        Lift me Jesus ! to Thy throne :

20. To my parting soul be given
      Entrance through the gate of heaven :
        There confess me for thine own !
                                        Amen.

Cor Jesu Sacratissimun.

* Cor Jesu Sacratissimun :
    Miserere nobis.
  Cor Mariæ Immaculatum,
   Ora pro nobis.

(To be sung three times.)

WITH HEARTS TRULY GRATEFUL.

1 With hearts truly grateful,
   Come all ye Faithful,
To Jesus, to Jesus in Bethlehem;
   See Christ your Saviour,
   Heaven's greatest favor.

     Let's hasten to adore Him;
     Let's hasten to adore Him;
     Let's hasten to adore Him;
      Our God and King.

2 God to God equal,
   Light to Light eternal:
Carried in Virgin's ever spotless womb;
   He all preceded,
   Begotten not created.

     Let's hasten, &c.

3 Angels now praise Him,
   Loud their voices raising,
The heavenly mansions with joy now ring,
   Praise, honor, glory,
   To Him who is most holy.

     Let's hasten, &c.

4 To Jesus born this day,
   Grateful homage repay;
To Him who all heavenly gifts doth bring,
   Word uncreated,
   To our flesh united.

     Let's hasten, &c.

HAIL VIRGIN OF VIRGINS.

1 Hail Virgin of Virgins,
   Thy praises we sing,
Thy Throne is in heaven,
   Thy Son is its king,
The saints and the angels
   Thy glory proclaim,
All nations devoutly
   Bow down at Thy name.

2 Let souls that are holy
   Still holier be,
To sing with the angels,
   Sweet Mary of thee.
Let all who are sinners
   To virtue return,
That hearts without number
   With thy love may burn.

3 Oh! be thou our Mother,
   And pray to the Lord.
That all may acknowledge
   And worship His word.
That good men with courage
   May walk in His ways,
And bad men converted,
   May join in His praise.   Amen.

HAIL, VIRGIN, DEAREST MARY.

1 Hail, Virgin, dearest Mary!
   Our lovely Queen of May;
O spotless, blessed lady,
   Our lovely Queen of May.

2 Thy children humbly bending
Around thy shrine so dear,
With heart and voice ascending—
Sweet Mary hear our prayer.
Hail, Virgin, &c.

3 Behold earth's blossoms springing,
In beauteous form and hue;
All nature gladly bringing
Her sweetest charms to you.
Hail, Virgin, &c.

4 We'll gather fresh, bright flowers,
To bind our fair Queen's brow;
From gay and verdant bowers,
We haste to crown thee now.
Hail, Virgin, &c.

5 And now, our blessed Mother,
Smile on our festal day,
Accept our wreath of flowers,
And be our Queen of May.
Hail, Virgin, &c.

MOTHER DEAR, O PRAY FOR ME.

1 Mother dear, O pray for me!
Whilst far from heav'n and thee,
I wander in a fragile bark,
O'er life's tempestuous sea!
O Virgin Mother, from thy throne,
So bright in bliss above,
Protect thy child and cheer my path,
With thy sweet smile of love.

Cho.—Mother dear, remember me,
    And never cease thy care,
'Till in heaven eterbally,
    Thy love and bliss I share.

2 Mother dear, O pray for me !
    Should pleasure's syren lay,
E'er tempt thy child to wander far
    From virtue's path away :
When thorns beset life's devious way;
    And darkling waters flow,
Then Mary, aid thy weeping child,
    Thyself a mother show.
      Mother dear, &c.

8 Mother dear, O pray for me !
    When all looks bright and fair,
That I may all my dangers see
    For surely then 'tis near ;
A Mother's prayer how much we need
    If prosperous be the ray,
That paints with gold the flow'ry mead,
    Which blossoms in our way.
      Mother dear, &c.

ON THIS DAY, O BEAUTIFUL MOTHER.

1 On this day, O beautiful Mother,
    On this day we give thee our love,
Near thee, Madouna, fondly we hover,
    Trusting thy gentle care to prove.

2 On this day we ask to share
    Dearest Mother, thy sweet care ;
Aid us ere our feet astray
    Wander from thy guiding way.
      On this day, &c.

3 Queen of angels, deign to hear,
  Lisping children's humble pray'r ;
  Young hearts gain, O Virgin pure,
  Sweetly to thyself allure.
    On this day, &c.

4 Rose of Sharon, lovely flow'r,
  Beauteous bud of Eden's bow'r ;
  Cherished lily of the vale,
  Virgin Mother, Queen we hail.
    On this day, &c.

5 In vain the flow'rs of love we bring,
  In vain sweet music's notes we sing,
  If contrite hearts and lowly prayers,
  Guide not our gifts to thy bright sphere
    On this day, &c.

6 Fast our days of life we run,
  Soon the night of death will come ;
  Tower of strength in that dread hour,
  Come with all thy gentle power.
    On this day, &c.

OH PARADISE.

Oh Paradise ! Oh Paradise !
  Who doth not crave for rest ?
Who would not seek the happy land
  Where they that loved are blest.
Oh Paradise ! Oh Paradise !
  This world is growing old :
Who would not be at rest and free,
  Where love is never cold.

2 O Paradise ! O Paradise !
   Wherefore doth death delay—
Bright death, that is the welcome dawn
   Of our eternal day ?
O Paradise ! O Paradise !
   'Tis weary waiting here ;
I long to be where Jesus is,
   To feel, to see Him near.

3 O Paradise ! O Paradise !
   I want to sin no more !
I want to be as pure on earth
   As on thy spotless shore.
O Paradise ! O Paradise !
   I greatly long to see
The special place my dearest Lord.
   Is furnishing for me.

Two Thousand Years Ago.

1 Two thousand years, two thousand years
   Our bark o'er billowy seas
Has onward kept her steady course
   Thro' hurricane and breeze ;
Her captain was the Risen one
   She braved the stormy foe.
And still He guides, who guided her
   Two thousand years ago.

2 When first our gallant ship was launched,
   Although our hands were few,
Yet dauntless was each bosom found,
   And every heart was true ;
And still though in her mighty hull
   Unnumbered bosoms glow,
Her crew is faithful as it was
   Two thousands years ago !

3 True, some had left this noble craft,
  To sail the seas alone,
And made them, in their hour of pride,
  A vessel of their own ;
· But, when portentous clouds did rise,
  Tempestuous storms did blow,
They re-eutered that old vessel built
  Two thousand years ago

4 For onward rides our gallant bark,
  With all her canvas set,
In some few nations still unknown
  To plant her standards yet :
Her flag shall float where'er a breath
  From human life shall glow,
And millions bless the bark that sailed
  Two thousand years ago.

5 True to that guiding star which led
  To Israel's cradled hope,
Her steady needle pointeth yet
  To Calvary's bloody top !
Yes! there she floats, that good old ship,
  From mast to keel below
Seaworthy still, as erst she was
  Two thousand years ago.

JESUS, MY LORD MY GOD.

1 Jesus, my Lord, my God, my all !
  How can I love Thee as I ought ?
And how revere this wondrous gift,
  So far surpassing hope or thought ?

Cho.—Sweet Sacrament ! we Thee adore,
  O make us love Thee more and more,
  O make us love Thee more and more.

2 Had I but Mary's sinless heart,
    To love Thee with, my dearest King,
O with what bursts of fervent praise,
    Thy goodness Jesus, would I sing !
·   Sweet Sacrament ! &c.

3 O see ! within a creature's hand,
    The vast Creator deigns to be,
Reposing, infant-like, as though
    On Joseph's arm, on Mary's knee !
    Sweet Sacrament ! &c.

4 Thy Body, Soul and Godhead, all
    O mystery of love divine !
I cannot compass all I have,
    For all Thou hast and art are mine !
    Sweet Sacrament ! &c.

———

AT THE COMMUNION.

1 O Lord I am not worthy
    That Thou shouldst come to me,
But speak the words of comfort,
    My spirit healed shall be.

2 And humbly I'll receive Thee,
    The Bridegroom of my soul,
No more by sin to grieve Thee,
    Or fly Thy sweet control.

O Jesus Remember.

1 O Jesus Christ remember
    When Thou shall come again,
Upon the clouds of heaven,
    With all Thy shining train,
When every eye shall see Thee,
    In Deity revealed,
Who now upon the altar
    In silence art concealed.

2 Remember then, O Saviour,
    I supplicate of Thee,
That here I bow'd before Thee,
    Upon my bended knee;
That here I own'd Thy Presence,
    And did not Thee deny,
And glorified Thy greatness,
    Though hid from human eye.

3 Accept, divine Redeemer,
    The homage of my praise;
Be Thou the light and honor
    And glory of my days;
Be Thou my consolation
    When death is drawing nigh:
Be Thou my only treasure
    Through all eternity.

DAILY, DAILY SING TO MARY.

1 Daily, Daily sing to Mary,
    Sing my soul her praises due,
All her feasts, her actions worship,
    With the heart's devotion true,
Lost in wondring contemplation,
    Be her majesty confessed;
Call her mother, call her Virgin,
    Happy Mother, Virgin blest.

2 She is mighty to deliver;
    Call her, trust her lovingly;
When the tempest rages round thee,
    She will calm the troubled sea.
Gifts of heaven she has given,
    Noble Lady, to our race;
She, the Queen, who decks her subjects
    With the light of God's own grace.

3 All my senses, heart, affections,
    Strive to sound her glory forth;
Spread abroad the sweet memorials
    Of the Virgin's priceless worth.
· Sing in songs of praise unending,
    Sing the world's majestic Queen;
Weary not, nor faint in telling
    All the gifts she gives to men.

ST. ANNE.

Spotless Anna! Juda's glory!
  Through the Church from East to West,
Every tongue proclaims thy praises,
  Mary's Mother blest!

CHORUS.

    Under thy protecting banner
      Here assembled in thy name,
    Mary's Mother, gracious Anna,
      Grace and help of thee we claim.

Saintly Kings and priestly Sires
  Blended in thy sacred line;
Thou in virtue all before thee
  Didst excel by grace divine.
      CHORUS.—Under thy, etc.

From thy stem in beauty budded
  Ancient Jesse's mystic rod;
Earth from thee received the Mother
  Of th' Almighty Son of God.
      CHORUS.—Under thy, etc.

All the human race benighted
  In the depths of darkness lay;
When in Anna, it saw the dawning
  Of the long-expected day.
      CHORUS.—Under thy, etc.

INDEX.